SO FAR SO GOOD

SO FAR SO GOOD

poems by
Mick Gowar

Illustrated by Barry Thorpe

COLLINS

William Collins Sons & Co Ltd
London · Glasgow · Sydney · Auckland
Toronto · Johannesburg

First published in 1986
© Mick Gowar 1986
Illustrations © Barry Thorpe 1986

British Library Cataloguing in Publication Data:
Gowar, Mick
  So far, so good.
  I. Title
  821´.914   PR6057.084/
  ISBN 0 00 184545-4 (hardback)
  ISBN 0 00 184414-8 (paperback)

Printed and bound in Great Britain
by Mackays of Chatham Ltd Kent

Contents

Acknowledgements

Of the poems in this book, the sequence 'First Love' and the two poems 'Hello, Goodbye' originally formed part of the screenplay for 'First Love', a television play commissioned by Anglia Television for the programme *Folio*; 'The Painter' was broadcast on BBC Schools Radio and first published in the accompanying notes to *Living Language*; and 'Dear Chicks' was originally published as a Cambridge Poetry Festival poster poem.

For Meg and her friends

King of the Kurzel

The Kurzel, Southend:
biggest loudest most
beautiful and brightest
gorgeous pleasure dome a
huge exploding crimson
blur electric blue a
whirling golden gleaming
jewel
sat by a sludge brown sea
All teeming human life left
miles and miles beneath:
   the biggest
everything in all the world.

The photograph is
black and white
it shows
two people
of about fourteen
in pale grey uniforms
one boy, one girl
The boy at first sight
seems to have a broken arm
around the girl
his hand a
curious limp epaulette
at her shoulder
his hand seems
scared, the intimacy
too much, too soon

they grin:
the girl has
both eyes lightly closed

the boy is me
the day was
it
the day of days
the outing of
the ATC and GVC
All month I'd prayed:
Oh, let her see me
don't let her see my nose, but
let her see me

I sat behind her
on the coach trip going down
appeared by chance
beside her
on the dipper
My dreams came true
She clutched my hand, clung,
held it harder when
the ride was over
kept on holding . . .
On the waltzer –
snaked my arm around her shoulders
She didn't shake it off
When we got off
hers wound itself
around my waist

(I couldn't breathe, believe it
never wanted such a joy
to end)

In the throng, that thrill
that thump, thump in my throat
So loud I'm sure she heard
my heart pound Oh, I love you

She kissed me on the coach
– not once, but over and over and over
And all the spinning, swirling
bucking bronco rides
were nothing, nothing like
    that
The coloured lights, the crowds
had witnessed
the great moment –
Me, grown-up
She'd shown them all
her lovely arms
around me
like a crown

Closing of the Door

God keep us safe this night,
Secure from all our fears,
May angels guard us while we sleep
Till morning light appears.
Amen.

A kiss, "Goodnight love, sleep tight, I'll
see you in the morning. Here's Dear-Dear and
your Teddy." Kiss; "Goodnight."

"Wait, *wait*,
No, *no*, *Auntie*, NO,
PLEASE
I never have the door shut I never have the light off
till I'm asleep, Auntie please, *please*, PLEASE –"

"WILL you be quiet.
I've never heard such a noise.
Why, you're a big boy now you go to school.
What noise, Good Heavens,
I've never heard such nonsense in all my life.
Now you just stop that,
right this minute.
What a baby, I don't know –
your father *will* be cross
when he comes home and hears
you've been *so* naughty!"

Naughty – what? who did she
mean? My Daddy never shuts the door,
he never turns my light out –

"Goodness Gracious,
will you *stop* that noise –
you'll wake your baby sister up,
she doesn't make a row like that."

The sounds grown softer, she goes downstairs.

When they came back –
an hour or so, no more –
Mummy heard him softly crying,
picked him up and soothed it all away:
brought him peace and warmth and quiet.
He knew then
the worst night of his life was over,
tomorrow was another happy day.

A kiss, "Don't worry, you can have your light on
all the time – as bright, as bright as any star,
as bright as anything you want. Here's Dear-Dear and
your Teddy." Kiss; "Goodnight."

He's sixteen now, and still remembers every word.

God keep us safe this night,
Secure from all our fears,
May angels guard us while we sleep
Till morning light appears.
Amen.

Pocket Money

"I can't explain what happens to my cash."
I can, but can't – not to my Mum and Dad.
"Give us 10p or get another bash" –

That's where it goes. And though their questions crash
Like blows, and though they're getting mad,
I can't explain what happens to my cash;

How can I tell the truth? I just rehash
Old lies. The others have and I'm the had:
"Give us 10p or get another bash."

"For dinner, Dad? . . . Just sausages and mash."
"That shouldn't make you broke by Wednesday, lad."
I can't explain. What happens to my cash? –

My friends all help themselves. I get the ash
Of fags I buy and give, get none. "Too bad.
Give us 10p or get another bash

For being you." And still I feel the thrash
Of stronger, firmer hands than mine; the sad
Disgust of living like a piece of trash.
I can't explain what happens to my cash.
"Give us 10p or get another bash."

An English Lesson

my Perfect Day

I

She daydreams:

A Lamborghini or a TR6 –
the coast road down to Monte Carlo or Loret.
The matching Gucci luggage in the boot;
my hand rests lightly on his neck.
His perfect suntanned features gleam,
his perfect pearl white teeth are set
in rugged concentration as – with perfect skill –
we purr down to his private beach
at Monte Carlo or Loret.

The snow lies crisp beneath the horses' hooves
and all the sleigh bells ring as we ride back –
up to his family chateau in the Alps.
He won the giant slalom while I clapped and clapped
    and clapped.
His perfect suntanned features gleam,
his perfect pearl white teeth are set
in rugged concentration as – with perfect skill –
we glide on through the snow. His castle towers gleam
like wedding cake with frosted icing capped.

And in our paradise of love,
he sweeps me gently from my feet,
he holds me in his fine strong arms and
covers me with countless kisses sweet.

His perfect suntanned features gleam,
his perfect pearl white teeth are set
in rugged concentration as – with perfect skill –
he makes the earth move time and time again
like pounding waves beneath my trembling feet.

II

He writes, then thinks:

My eggs and bacon cooked the way I like –
the bacon crisp and crackling underneath the fork,
the hot fat spooned across the white.

The River Orwell at the crack of dawn –
the shadows long and sunlight sparkling fresh,
the first fat roaches nuzzling the bait.

Wembley: in extra time and still no score –
a long ball arcing through the biting air
splits the defence – the full-back high and dry,

the chip inside: I hit the perfect volley
on the turn . . . a micro-second's silence
smashed as 50,000 fans go wild.

(That looks all right.
The truth is,
if I had all that
I'd give it all for
just one
smile
from
Her.)

Dear 'Chicks'

I spend a lot of time, well,
not afraid – not fear so much
– worried. It's not stupid,
My Mum and Dad don't know, they say
it's stupid; but that's because
they just don't know. In their day
it was easy getting mates – they still
come round, all their old mates from school
for drinks and things.
But it's not the same, not
now it's not; and I don't know
what I'd do if
one day I woke up
and didn't have no mates.
They just don't know how hard it is.

The other day, your magazine, it
had this quiz: "Are You the Sort the Other
Girls Want to be With? – Find Out!"
I got all the answers wrong – I couldn't move,
I couldn't breathe,
I didn't *know!*

And in this other magazine
it had this other quiz on clothes and
all about "Do You Look Good Enough
To Want To Have Around?" And God,
I didn't have, well, hardly none of it.
And Dad, he doesn't listen when I tell,
I tell him and he just gets really mad;
and Mum won't do my skirt.
Look, I said, I can't, I can't go into school
like *that*.
And Mum gets cross,
I try and tell her,
time and time again, I really try.
Then Dad says, "Can't? You *can't?*
Oh yes, you can, you WILL!"

So please don't print this letter, 'cos
if all my mates found out
I don't know what I'd do.

But if you could
please, please write back –
It's just that I don't know what to do
And you're the only one who understands.

Oh Yeah?

Every day I come in good as gold,
I've got them fooled – they can't catch me!
Yes, I'll listen – but I won't be told.
Every day I come in good as gold,
Register . . . then disappear. I'm free!
Every day I come in good as gold,
I've got them fooled – they can't catch me!

Engaged Tone

I've been ringing that number again and again
and again and again and *again* and AGAIN
And each time I listen it happens again,
If it does it once more
I'll go effing insane,
Six-seven one-seven-nine-seven-four –
Neurh . . . neurh . . . neurh . . . neurh.

I'll go for a walk, no
I'll go for a SCREAM –
It must be a nightmare
(it isn't a dream),
It's got all the ingredients:
Horror, Suspense and
a Monster that howls like a cat on a fence or
the shriek of a Banshee tormenting its prey –
Neurh . . . neurh ... neurh . . . neurh . . .

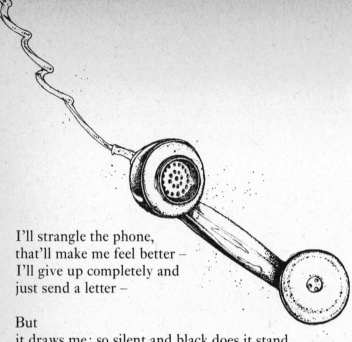

I'll strangle the phone,
that'll make me feel better –
I'll give up completely and
just send a letter –

But
it draws me: so silent and black does it stand
and it fits itself snugly right into my hand –
if I try *just once* more . . .

Oh God! I can't bear it –
I'll smash it!
I'll drown it!
I'll hack it!
I'll tear it!

I could try all day *long*
I could try for a *year*
it would still be the same sound
– still loud and still clear – of
that shrill vile thing being
sick in my ear

Neurh . . . neurh . . . neurh . . . neurh . . . neurh . . .
     neurh . . . neurh . . .

A Day at the Beach

1 *The Father's Tale*

God Almighty! What a trip!
Two and a half hours on the bypass
then the B3569 jam-packed
and I thought that'd speed things up –
a short cut? Huh! There are times I'd like to go
screaming past them all,
smash the pedal through the floor
and push the bastards off the road.
As if that's not enough
the Ayatollah's right beside me
jabbering nineteen to the dozen,
"Told you so. We should have got
an earlier start, it's always
like this, every year,
you ought to know by now."
Then up pipes Tracey,
"Oh Dad, how much longer
are we going to be stuck here?"
So I flip me wig
"*Shut up*. Just SHUT UP, both of you!"
"Yes, be quiet Tracey,
can't you see
your father's trying to concentrate."
There are times, I swear,
when I could murder her.

We finally arrive. Guess what?
All the deckchairs gone
so everyone's jammed in together
on the beach,
and some fool barking through a hailer
Not to swim far out.
So even in the blasted sea
we're nose to tail.

And then,
to cap it all,
Her Royal Highness
Princess Tracey
(who it's all been for) announces
calm as you please
she won't be going in:
"Don't want to!"
Doesn't want to get her swimsuit wet,
her hair messed up,
or some such bloody nonsense, I suppose.
So what do you think we do?
We sit there like a load of puddin's
looking out to sea,
while all around us

all humanity is screaming at its kids:
"Do that again and
your Dad'll give you such a belt!"
Call that having fun?
I've had more pleasure from a toothache!

It took four hours getting back –
can't even bear to think about it . . .
What? No, no,
My round this time, OK?
Yes – when you're ready, Jack,
the same again and
could I have a pack of
small cigars?

It really makes me angry
having him so cross and snappy
with us.
All the way down
– and all the way back.
I said, it's not *my* fault
the traffic's awful.
I don't know why we bother –
every year's the same
he's got to check
the oil, the water,
heaven knows what else. And so
we're still waiting to get off at
Half Past Eight!

We really only do it now for Tracey.
She used to love it there when she was little,
but now of course she's getting, well,
mature – too old for all that stuff . . .
You what?
No, not yet, thank God,
she hasn't started yet. Although,
I must admit, when she said
she didn't want to go in swimming!
Well, she's usually so keen. I thought
well, maybe that's the reason.
But it wasn't. I suppose
it's just her age. You know, they get so
lazy, always saying "Boring".
Everything's "Boring".
Ooh, I hate that –
Telly – "Boring".
Reading – "Boring".

To make things worse,
half way through the afternoon
they bring this body up the beach.
No, we didn't actually see it. But,
you know, it could have really
spoilt the day.
You'd think they could have waited,
at least until we'd all gone home.
It's not right, not with
children on the beach,
that sort of thing.

Anyway, we didn't stay much longer.
Well, with Tracey all pernickety and
him getting all worked up with
the driving back
there wasn't really much
to stay for,
was there?

3 *The Daughter's Tale*

Diary: Saturday, June 30, 11.30
The Worst Day Of My Life

Started off
us going down the sea
– Dead Boring –
Them at each other
all the way down: nag, nag, nag
so I just say
nothing,
keep quiet,
stay out of it.

We get there,
sit down on the beach and
I hear these people
talking about
there's been an accident,
a man drowned,
and just beyond the swimmers
two boats criss-crossing
back and forth
back and forth

And I have this sort of
funny dream, where
it's Mum that has the accident, and
Dad and I go to the water's edge and
I'm so brave and
hold him tightly while he cries
But I don't cry
And later we have to look
at her body
Dad can't look, but I can
And everybody says,
Isn't she brave?
And I go out to work
and he stays home
and nurses a broken heart
and every day I come home
cook the meals and everything
being brave enough for both of us
and all the neighbours say,
Isn't she brave
you'd never guess
just to look at her,
how brave she can be –
What a Wonderful Girl.

And then I see
the boats again,
someone staring down
into the water and
Mum says, "Aren't you going
swimming, love?"
That's when I realised
what I'd done: I'd
wanted her to die!
I never felt so awful
in all my life before.

And I hear myself say,
"Yes, Mum"; see myself
swim out, not far
and feel
the dead hands clutch my legs,
see it rise like a balloon,
see its eyes bulge out –
its grinning mouth,
see it
drag me under

And I know he's there
now, waiting for

me

Growing Pains

The twelfth of August.
The sun-baked ground brown concrete,
the yellow grass sparse hair
on an old woman's head.

Ants like freckles
twitch between the thin wisps:
everybody lies and gasps
– except my father.

Swollen with energy he capers,
bulgy over crimson boxer shorts:
I cringe behind the apple tree –
how stupid he looks.

How childish he is:
how *could* he?
What if someone sees him
dressed like that –

gambolling like a loon,
all flab and chest hair,
long short grey socks and rubber flip-flops.
Oblivious – so childish, childish.

Then Dad lifts the rabbit from its run
and trots around the garden,
the big black buck held firm
against his naked chest,

giving it a guided tour – "These are
the cabbages – yum, yum – and there, the goozygogs . . ."
My Mum, flat out beneath the William pear,
sees danger: "Do be careful, dear.

If Sooty jumps – you know how strong
his back legs are." My Dad
stares into the rabbit's eyes,
"He wouldn't hurt his Daddy,
                                    would he?"

The rabbit, bored with being Bunny,
leaps free. Kicking back,
his claws leave four great
bleeding weals across my father's chest.

My mother crows and leads the way
indoors to bathe the wounds in antiseptic.
Serves him right for being so daft.
Me, so much more adult,

embarrassed, bored and cross
beneath the tree –
serves him right, serves him right,
serves him right.

From somewhere in the house
I hear a bellow
as the antiseptic stings.
Big baby.

A Man About the House

Sunday morning, rain last night.
Jack stayed over, once again –
a leak came through the ceiling
into Mum's room.

This morning, after breakfast,
I was organized to help
Jack climb up
into the loft to fix it.

He stuck fast
(I could see he would) –
his fat red bum in dungarees
plugged the trap.

Stuck straining on the highest step,
the ladder shuddering –
pushing, sweating,
muffled groans:

"What kind of pillock
builds a trap
a midget couldn't . . . "
In the end he gave up – held the torch:

I climbed the ladder
gripped the edge
swung up and through –
(Easy! Easy! Easy!)

"Now you be careful . . .!"
Crawling out along the joists I felt
so good: like a commando
or the SAS (crouched out of sight)

while down below, Jack
waved the torch about
and shouted orders much too loud.
I knew what to do.

Up above me lay the tiles
like slapped palms, slits
of light like knife glints
in between.

From my pocket take
the torch Dad gave me,
search the beams
and there

in the fur crust dust
the tell-tale, tiny
snail trail of water
slithering down.

Snap off the torch,
come down the steps.
"There's no sign of a leak up there, Jack."
Puzzled look: "You sure?"

"Yeah. Nothing there at all."
Another look, suspicious,
(whisper) "Go on – take a look yourself
if you don't believe me . . ."

Song

Here.
To be
warm and quiet,
   alone,
      myself,
         quite separate.

Let them
(below)
crash bang and bellow,
row and bawl –
                   I'll

                     Stay
                     right here
                     upstairs

                         myself
                         alone
                         quite separate.

Space Invader

I knifed him 'cos he bugged me
– can't you understand
nothing? Look:

I was on Level 4 – Right.
God, when you get to
Level 4, you know

Nobody, but Nobody
gives you any
hassle – Right?

No? Jeez–us
You're so, you know –
Dense!

I'll do it
all again,
So *listen:*

I was in the
Arcade –
Right?

Just zapped the
Flyers
then – oh God,

What A Day! –
I creamed the
Mother-Ship

Total. So now it's
Level 4 –
Right?

That's when he
tugs my sleeve –
Right?

And so I
stuck him –
Right?

And got on with the game.

So now you see,
It stands to reason.
Anyone would do the same

Guitarist

It looks so easy on the telly
watching all the bands in concert.
Why, then, do *my* fingers always
tie themselves in knots?

Why do I have to use *both* hands
(the one I'm s'pposed to strum with, too)
to force my fingers into D
every single time?

I watch them on the video
all poncing, prancing, waggling bums;
there's no long gaps when *they* change chords.
– How come?

How is it they can sing in tune,
and leap about, *and* strut and pout,
and change from E flat to G seventh
all at once?

How come *they* never have to look,
they never have to count the frets
to try and work out where it all went
wrong . . . again?

I've practiced every night for *weeks*,
I've even bought a tutor book:
so why, oh why am I still stuck on
Bobby sodding Shaftoe?

My Kid Brother

Not picked for chain–he,
squatting on the low wall
two bricks high
around the flower bed
around the tree,
scuffing the loose gravel:
builds a pile between his feet

Mutters to himself as though absorbed
picks
at the moss
between the bricks
between his knees
pick pick pick don't look
pick pick pick don't look up

A lone ant crawls too near,
he crunches it;
throws back his head –
Punched by the flashbulb sun
the water floods his eyes
but still his hands attack
the moss
head down he clears
a . . . drainage ditch?
between the bricks

with total
concentration. No-
one asks the question,
                    "What you doing?"

Anyone can see
he didn't want to play
that game:
got plenty better things
to do

pick
pick pick
pick pick pick

Alsoran

Your chest hurts twice as bad,
your legs weigh twice as much
when you're alone, adrift
and twenty yards behind the pack.

That special pain that creeps
from chest to shoulder, stabs
beneath the collar bone
and drains all energy away.

Why keep going why keep
thumping on through thick and
thin can't think can't
hardly breathe can't

catch them up can't
keep it up can't
give up now can't face the end
can't win can't stop can't

With easy flowing strides the Blond God
laps you saps
each last despairing flailing
ounce of energy each

Smooth as a tank he glides –
Head Boy next year,
a Scholarship the next and
here, this afternoon, the 1500 metres.

He stands beside the finish being sporting –
the tape sliced,
clean as a whistle,
his from the starting gun:

he's hardly damp. You're sweating like a pig,
wheezing like a broken mattress;
you stagger to a stop,
fall on your knees and puke your dinner up.

With sympathetic smile, he
nimbly skips aside;
you labour on,
his running shoes unsoiled.

Spiggott

1 On the Boil

Spiggott thinks he's scored
– all the way –
Jeanette
Due to meet behind
the Long Jump pit:
the opportunity of
a lifetime. Unable to resist,
he's told a few close mates;
a lot of other people seem to know.

Lunchtime:
jogging (casually) he's
right on time, he's
round the corner of the Old Block,
past the sheds, he's passed
the hydrangeas,
down the steps,
along the covered way and
round the corner of the gym
he's
    Intercepted

"OK Spiggott, what's the hurry?"
Fingers sliding down his greasy collar
he panics – empties out his pockets,
petrified of being late – "Here,
take the lot –"
No time to argue:
money, toffees, wrappers, paper clips,
a leaking cartridge.
For the first time in
their criminal careers, the Jack the Lads are
dumbstruck

Spiggott sprints
down to the High Jump pit,
he finds

> – deserted
> no-one
> nothing

High on the top floor
of the bright new block
the telescope from Physics 2
wrenched from hand to hand,
the hot air saturated with *Impulse* and *Frenzy*,
pierced by the razor screams
of girlish laughter
(We all cracked up,
we couldn't help it,
could we?)

And Oh, the first of
many long walks back before the braying caws
                              of Gym Club smokers

2 *Under a Bushel*

In Love
again, Spiggott is taking
no chances –
spending a lot of time with
his head in his desk, keeping
his raspberry pitted profile
very low.

In the darkness
life is pretty seedy:
Spiggott excavates
a homework record-book –
empty, infused with the sweet stench of
a crusted dung-brown apple core;
dust lies snow-deep
over the shrapnelled forest litter:
gnawed pencil splinters, shattered
biro tubes;
the masticated paper globs of ancient gooly bombs
pickle the debris.

Spiggott's teeth,
white, regular, exercised to a
peak of fitness
gleam beautifully, but
hidden, secret and invisible.

3 *Over the Top*

Geraldine is not
the most
beautiful girl in the world, but
to Spiggott's eyes she has
possibilities. She seems to like him,
he likes her, but neither of them certain:
both dream of something better, but till then . . .
things could be worse.

They snuggle down.
Below, the music pounds;
among the coats they kiss
enthusiastically although
teeth get in the way
from time to time.
A digital alarm clock
carefully placed shows
five more minutes.

With several weeks established, both
attempt to ease off
the clinging dress –
it sticks.
He pushes down –
it knots,
a zip-jammed bundle
barricading at the waist.
They both stand: lips pursed,
wriggling,
two more minutes on the clock.
With thirty seconds left it's
far too late,
the effort pointless.

Hurriedly, and back to back, adjust
the slight disorders in their dress.
He wonders as they make their way downstairs
(and leave the room to others in the queue)
however did she manage to get on – alone –
a dress that *both* of them could not undo?

Media Studies

She is my homework for tonight.
My Media Studies project's nearly done,
I've nearly filled my folder, but a bit
From *Panorama* always gets you extra marks.

I switch on at the part the trailer showed –
A girl like me, but younger, "in the club".
She fidgets in the posh chrome/leather chair –
So small her feet don't reach the floor.

She says: "I want someone to love me, only me
More than anyone else in all the world."
Her boyfriend's far too young to marry, and besides
She doesn't really like him any more.

The baby's all she wants, and that's enough.
She knows for sure the kind of life they'll share –
She won't be like a Mum, they'll grow up mates
And both go down the Disco Saturday night.

She knows, just knows it's going to be a girl.
She'll call her Carly, dress her up real nice
Look after her and that, all on her own.
She talks as if a baby's just a doll!

It's later, trying to write it up – I can't explain . . .
But somehow, what I mean is that it's wrong
To show it all on telly, wrong to pry –
What did she know? She's just a kid – that's all.

How can I put it in my folder, get it marked?
It's someone's life, how can you grade that B or C?
Is that all that her interview was for –
A pass or fail in someone else's CSE . . .?

Hello, Goodbye

I

I used to be the one who led the way,
Who made the running, who was in control:
"It's much too soon for us to get tied down" –
And so we split up for a month or two.
And now I hear the same things said by her,
"We're getting too intense, let's cool things off . . ."

I'm now the weak one and she's in control
(As one goes up, the other's sinking down),
Now I must compromise enough for two –
Trying each day to make amends to her,
To prove I love her, trying to fend off
That awful moment when she walks away.

It's slipping by, like condensation down
A window pane. How long? . . . a week, or two,
A day? The whole thing's up to her –
I'm barely coping, fighting to put off
The end, still struggling to find a way
To win her back and try to keep control

Of my self from day to day. Do just two
Minutes pass not filled with thoughts of her?
No. Loving like this is work with no time off –
Each second spent in planning out a way
To act quite natural, cool and in control;
To show I'm still the one she wants, deep down.

I dread each moment when I'm not with her;
Call every hour on the phone, ring off . . .
Something I said – she might take the wrong way!
Call back to check, make sure – out of control,
In quicksand, each step sinking deeper down.
"Look, can't you let it rest? It's only two

More hours to the party – surely two
Hours isn't much. I'm meeting Jane, her
Dad will drive us there. Meet you at the Off-
Licence on the corner. You know the way?
I'll see you there. And do try to control
The boozing, please. Try not to let me down."

Her phone goes down. I must have self-control . . .
"Yes . . . don't ring off – Could Jane's Dad's car
     take two –
I'll come with you . . . I won't be in the way? . . ."

II

"I wanted just to gently let it go,
A gradual split. I said: Let's take a break,
Just for a while. I need some space to grow
In different ways. Look, for heaven's sake
We shouldn't see each other *every* night,
There's other people that I want to be
With – friends, for instance. Don't you think I'm right?
He broke down like a child and clung to me:
He sobbed his heart out. What was I to do?
I gave in straight away, but since that day
As far as I'm concerned – that's it. We're through.
You've no idea how good it is to say
All this to you – you really understand . . ."
He's thinking: Next step – try to hold her hand!

Teaching Practice

Thwack! "Go on, get out of here, and don't come back!
. . . I treat them all like that, that's all they understand –
And they respect you for it, mark my words.
In forty years *I've* never had a rowdy class – not once!

Forget that nonsense that they teach you in your
Education Course. Those lecturers don't know the score,
The simple fact that most kids just aren't human beings
          at all,
They're animals. They don't respond to kindness, trust –

A whip and chair is more their mark. You've got to scare
The little brutes. Yes, scare them rigid, make them live
In fear of you. That's discipline . . .

Hey – *You!* . . . Did you see that? The little beast
          was spying,
Listening to every word I've said. Go on – yes, run!
Quick! . . . Bring him back. – See me tomorrow morning,
          after play. –
That's how it's done! You're learning fast –
  you'll be all right."

Hero

"Of course I took the drugs. Look, son,
there's no fair play, no gentlemen,
no amateurs, just winning.
How old are you? Fifteen? Well,
you should know that
no one runs for fun – well, not beyond
the schoolboy stuff – eleven or twelve years old.
I'd been a pro for years;
my job – to get that Gold.

Mind you, we English are an odd lot:
like to believe we love the slob that fails,
the gentlemanly third; so any gap-toothed yob who
                              gets the glory
also gets some gentlemanly trait: helps cripples get across
the street, nice to small animals. You know the kind of thing,
it helps the public feel it's
all legit; that sportsmanship is real and that
it's all clean fun –
the strongest, bravest, fittest
best man won.

Yeah, Steroids . . . Who do *you* think? . . . Oh,
                              don't be wet –
My coach, of course, he used to get them
through this vet . . . The side effects? Well, not so bad
as these things go – for eighteen months or so
I didn't have much use for girls. But, by then I
                              was training
for the Big One – got to keep the body pure,
not waste an ounce of effort."

He gives a great guffaw.
A chain of spittle
rattles down the front of
his pyjama jacket.
He wipes his mouth;
His eyes don't laugh at all.

". . . Do it again? Of course I would –
I'd cheat, I'd box, I'd spike, I'd pay the devil's price
to be that good again
for just one day. You see, at twenty-three
I peaked – got all I ever wanted:
all anyone would ever want from me.
After the race, this interviewer told me
Fifty million people's hopes and dreams had been
fulfilled – a Gold!
How many ever get that chance? I did.
Would you say No to that?
Of course not.

Damn, the bell. You'd better go, they're pretty strict.
Yeah, leave the flowers there on the top,
the nurse'll get some water and a vase."

YTS Introduction

(Today is the first day of Induction. Yesterday
Was applications; tomorrow, sorting out the placements.
Packed like seedlings into a room above the works canteen –
Blue plastic folders full of printed sheets and forms –
Six to a table.) "Find yourselves a place, please . . . Right,
Is everybody here? . . . Then I'll begin.

"Good morning lads – and girls . . . and welcome.
My name is Squadron Leader, sorry, *Mr* Trench (forgot!)
– We're all new boys together, eh? Ha-ha . . .
As I was saying, lads, this year will give you all
The skills you'll need in adult life. I will explain:
Look at the sheets provided – heading,
     Outline of the Course.

"To help develop your awareness of your Self
. . . er, self-satisfaction, admiration, all that stuff . . .
You will have Personal Effectiveness
     for two hours every week
For three weeks – starting in a minute. This will
Be followed by your first, informal, Self-Assessment –
Which will be new to most of you, of course.

"During the year we've Dealing with the Public,
Self-Presentation, Telephone Enquiries, Letters;
Planning and Problem-Solving, Communications and
When and Where to Use Initiative . . . Oh, and
Those of you in Caring Skills will have
How to Deal with Children, in addition.

"That brings us to Computers. Writing your
                                        own programs
In Basic will be covered by the course. Unfortunately,
Your training programme won't include Pascal,
Which, in the case of our machines, they have not got.
This module is called Computer Literacy and will
Be followed by Computer Self-Assessment.

Ignore Page 5 . . . Go on to Section 7.
We come at last, then, to the Final Project.
This will involve the Skills of Organizing, Finding Facts,
The Need for Accuracy, and, if there's time,
You'll have the chance to *duplicate, collate* and *bind* them
All yourselves! Before, of course, your
    Final Self-Assessment.

"Any questions? . . . Good. If everybody's ready
I'll begin . . ."

(Today is the first day of Induction. Yesterday
Was applications; tomorrow, sorting out the placements.
Packed like seedlings into the room above
                                        the works canteen –
Blue plastic folders full of printed sheets and forms –
Six to a table . . .)

End of the Line

Three days of solid rain
like ropes, three days and nights.
The building site was like a marsh,
a quagmire full of sudden holes and pits:
a death-trap.

In the hut the three men
simmered in their own foul air –
Joe's sweat, Tom's constant roll-ups
and the fetid stench of stale milk,
the hangover of three days' cups of
strong, sweet tea
brewed by Gary every hour
on the hour, regular as clockwork.
The only conversation
snaps and snarls and
"Sod you, Joe."

Bill (site manager),
stuck inside the site-hut,
muttered curses at the rain.
His hut was like a railway tea-bar
in a train strike –
one long queue of moan, moan, moan.
First the boss
and then the architect
and then the both of them.

Always the same old story:
"If you don't get the drains in
by the weekend
there'll be hell to pay,
And you'll be paying."
He'd gone down to the tin hut,
told Joe his fortune
with a few selected *fs* and *bs*.
Hadn't stopped the rain
but Bill was feeling better.

Suddenly, at ten to twelve,
it stopped.
The three men sloshed out through the mud
to where the trenches had been dug.
"Oh God," thought Joe, "it can't be done."
Then he remembered all the things that
Bill had said –
how Joe was only put in charge on trial,
and how this job was due to finish –
if and when the drains went in.
No guarantee of any work next month,
specially not for foremen that
weren't up to scratch.

Eh?
Nasty, that.
"Right, Tom, get down that hole and
get stuck in."
Good management, thought Joe:
clear, firm and always in control.
"Naff off!" said Tom.
"You'd need to be a sewer rat to work
down there. Send Gary down,
that's what we've got these youngsters for."

Joe wasn't bright,
he wasn't brave:
a man like Tom said *No* just once.
Ask twice –
you'd have to push your toothbrush
down your throat to
clean your teeth.
"You heard him, Gary, down you go."
"But Joe, it ain't shored up yet –"
"Listen, lad, you're not here to argue,
Remember.
Four whole weeks you've been here and
can't even brew a decent cup of tea.
If you don't want your cards, right now,
you'll get straight down that hole and start."

Gary liked it on the site. (Sitting with
the men
in the tin hut made him feel
great, like
mates.)

He climbed down, started digging.

Ten minutes later
Gary heard the sound of thunder
right beside him,
opened up his mouth to scream –
it filled with thick black ooze.
The darkness slithered in
and crushed him flat.

It took an hour and a half to dig
the body out.
They closed the site down
for the day,
out of respect.

The Blind Eye of the Little Sony God

There's a teak-topped, square-eyed idol standing silent
                                             in the room
Flanked by faces stained with tears and scarred with frowns,
Each a mask of desperation, each despairing of salvation
On that dreadful night the TV set broke down.

Ever since the world began we've had tea with ITN –
All the food on trays and balanced on our knees.
'Cos our Dad must have his soup seasoned with the
                                             latest coup,
All the murders, deaths and famine and disease.

While the regions' magazines are on we're chomping on
                                             our greens,
Then we have a little Crossroads with the meat;
And in the advertising slot Mum is up and like a shot
Dishes out our bowls of Coronation Sweet.

All the programmes looked quite normal on that black
                                        and dreadful night
(Though the weatherman had mauve streaks in his hair);
When the TV set rolled over, stuck its back legs in the air,
We were on our marks for Jeux sans Frontieres –

So at first we didn't realize the dire and dreadful truth:
We thought the lack of picture and of sound
Was because that nice presenter (who was dressed up
                                        as a melon)
Had fallen in the swimming pool and drowned.

Then – as slowly as the sun sets or the white dot disappears,
And as softly as the dropping of a pin,
The final strains of It's a Knockout gently faded from
                                        our ears
And the awful darkness started closing in.

Waves of horror, waves of panic swept across each
                                    startled face
And like drowning men who seize at any clump
Of projecting vegetation, we set to – no hesitation –
It was "Action Stations! All hands to the pump!"

First my Mum dialled 999, but was too upset to speak,
Then my Dad tried all the First Aid he had learned:
He tried splints and sticking plaster – then, to add to
                                    our disaster,
Tried the kiss of life and got quite badly burned.

Then my Granny tried the remedy that always works for her
Grabbed the bottle from her armchair by the fire –
Tipped a king-size gin and tonic down the horizontal hold
And the poor set gave one splutter and expired.

There's a silent square-eyed idol in the corner of the room,
There's a heavy cloud of desperation there;
Where there once was joy and laughter, only gloom and
                                    frazzled nerves
And the smell of burnt transistors in the air.

The Painter

She has a hidden eye
behind her eyes
that sees in drab brown fields
    lush, purple pie-crust corduroy; a river
    swishing as a tiger's tail of pink and gold.

A rook hops, bops and
meddles through its
private rooky day –
    she fixes him. A brooding shadow casts
    an eerie chill across the middle ground.

For storm grey skies
she captures
    livid greens blood reds and
    fearful nightmare blacks;
I look and shudder
    somewhere deep inside
    a frightened creature wakes.

Her paintings speak in shapes and colours
I can never see, but know are true:
I try to paint the things I see
    but she can see the things she paints –
    she has the gift, the second sight
    to make things new.

First Love

Beginning

He remembers:

Both waiting for the bus, a 102,
dank miserable November air
like a sore throat
swathed in tattered scarves of wispy fog.
You stare ahead, your fingers blue and numb with cold
(no inkling of how much I care).

So much in love with you,
in such despair –
to dare to take this chance to
speak, to . . .
(but your beauty strikes me dumb and
I can only stare – too close,
too near)
        The bus is overdue!
Awoken by the certainty of losing you
a sudden rush of courage stammers:
Share my coat, it's
plenty big enough for two to . . .

Then you laugh, and
(blessed sweet rare and precious miracle)
you plunge your freezing hand
into the deep blue velvet pocket,
link your icy fingers through
my own.

(And in that moment
all my dreams come true.)

II

She:

I'd caught you weeks before: one look
too many and your cover blown – the clumsy spy
darting back behind your book
(Your serious face and private eyes).
Each time I turned my head to look
at you – too slow to hide, too quick
for me to catch your eye and say
   "I know, I know – I'm glad! I know!"

I'd watched you watching me;
I'd watched you trying not to let it show:
each time I turned round – there you'd be
trying to look the other way (but just a bit too slow).
Why did you take so long? Why? Didn't you know
that I was watching too?
   I know you know I know you know I know!

III

Waiting

She:

Every wheel you can hear
on George the Fifth Avenue
can stop your heart dead;
but none of them slow,
make the turn by the holly tree –

One car,
only one car
in the whole world
rushing past
time and again and again

Shush, shush, shush –

But don't look
out of the window,
or the car won't start;
don't ache for him so
or he'll never turn up

Just listen,
listen to the wet road

Come to me,
please, please come to me
Just come –
nothing else, you don't
even have to
talk to me

Only come, and I'll

Love You
Forever

IV

First Light

Alone – so strange to feel so all alone
when she lies here, beside me
in the deep blue bed

Transformed, unrecognizable in sleep.
The face I've gazed at, studied
every changing mood:

I wanted this so much.
Yesterday, last week, last month, last year
my whole life waiting

For this, one night
and now it's nearly over.
Daybreak.

The window's clearing to an oily grey;
a fragment of a song keeps going
round and round and round my head;

Get up once again (so quiet
she doesn't stir)
walk to the window once again.

The world lies dead outside.
The milk float's clatter and
the scratching cry of birds

Echo, echo without end;
What happens, happens now:
Where do we go from here?

V

He doodles a love poem, then
tears it up:

Oh love, how can I even
glance at you –
when every movement,
just the slightest turning of your head
sends shivers down my spine
and makes me dream of
Bed.

VI

A few weeks later

She:

I don't know why, but something's going wrong –
I felt the point of no return slip by.
Though we're still happy, we still get along

my heart beats like a toneless leaden gong
where once it leapt and raced as if to fly.
I don't know why. But something's going wrong

in me: the spark, the naturalness has gone –
each day it's getting harder to deny;
though we're still happy, we still get along

I'm out of step. He hasn't changed. How long
each kiss feels with deceit; each touch a lie.
I don't know why, but something's going wrong.

I'd never felt such love – so fierce and strong:
each sight of him, each parting made me cry.
Though we're still happy, we still get along

the love that was to last a whole life long
is coming to an end. No second try,
though we're still happy, we still get along.
I don't know why, but something's going wrong.

VII

I knew it had to come. I couldn't bear
it then; can't take it now. I'll make amends.
I'm willing to agree, now. So – be fair,
there's no need to split up. We'll just be friends.
Like you suggested. Not see quite so much
of each other. Please! I agree. You're right.
I made too much of what we had. Been such
a fool. I'll take the blame. We'll start tonight
– The New Improved Regime. We'll both be free
to do just as we want – the adult way.
I'll do just as you want me to. You'll see.
I'm willing to do anything you say.
I promise. I won't make a scene. Won't cry.
If you'll do just one thing. Don't say goodbye.

VIII

"I know I said we'd have another try;
I'm sorry, but I can't go on this way,
Pretending we're just fine – it's all a lie –
So let's be honest, let's call it a day.
For heaven's sake, don't look at me like that –
You chucked me once before, don't you recall?
I won't forget – night after night I sat
Beside the phone just waiting for your call.
There's no one else: I want to take a break.
What? Put myself through that again? No way;
I'm sorry, but I've lost the will to fake
– I couldn't stand it for another day."

   I saw her later on my best friend's knee,
   And kissing for the whole damn world to see.